# 100 HUGS

# 100 HUGS
## (a little book of comfort)

### Sandy gingras

**Andrews McMeel
Publishing, LLC**

Kansas City · Sydney · London

Andrews McMeel Publishing, LLC
an Andrews McMeel Universal company
1130 Walnut Street, Kansas City, Missouri 64106

www.andrewsmcmeel.com
www.how-to-live.com

13 14 15 16 17 SDB 10 9 8 7 6 5 4 3 2 1

ISBN: 978-1-4494-2729-0

Library of Congress Control Number: 2013931314

ATTENTION: SCHOOLS AND BUSINESSES

Andrews McMeel books are available at quantity discounts
with bulk purchase for educational, business, or sales
promotional use. For information, please e-mail the
Andrews McMeel Publishing Special Sales Department:
specialsales@amuniversal.com

# 100 HUGS

We all need hugs, because life is hard. Sometimes, a hug seems like a small thing compared to the troubles we face.

It can feel Like a drop in a very deep bucket.

But every hug is a mini-healing, a mini-affirmation, a mini-step-in-the-right-direction.

And even the smallest things
add up to something, if
we let them...

This book is to remind you that hugs are everywhere — in moments, in gestures, in cozy chairs and kind words, in milkshakes and mountain breezes— within your grasp.

Even when you feel alone, you are surrounded by hugs. Here are one hundred for you...

eating

oodles of
noodles

carbohydrates

1

2 being listened to
(and really heard)

3 wearing

an old flannel shirt
(soft and full of warm memories)

5 wearing fuzzy socks

6 smelling a wood fire on a crisp autumn day

7 the phrase: "This too shall pass..."

8 being in an herb garden full of butterflies
LAVEN
SAGE
Chives
BASIL

**9** humming to yourself
(also singing and whistling—
even if badly)

**10** getting a pedicure in
a vibrating
chair

**11** a stranger holding the door for you

**12** seeing the first signs of spring

**13** getting the corner booth

**14**

hearing an old song on the radio and remembering...

15 being creative

16 taking a deep
   cleansing breath

17 soaking in
a lovely bath

18 beachcombing

19 sleeping on crisp clean sheets

**20**

Lighting the fancy
candle for yourself

**21** Licking the
bowl

**22** getting in your jammies early

**23** stringing white twinKLe Lights in the summer trees

# 24 blowing kisses

# 25 Licking around the edges of an ice cream cone

**26** tasting the first bite of cinnamon toast

**27** saying the word: **"YAY"** about life

**28** feeling the touch of morning sunlight on your face

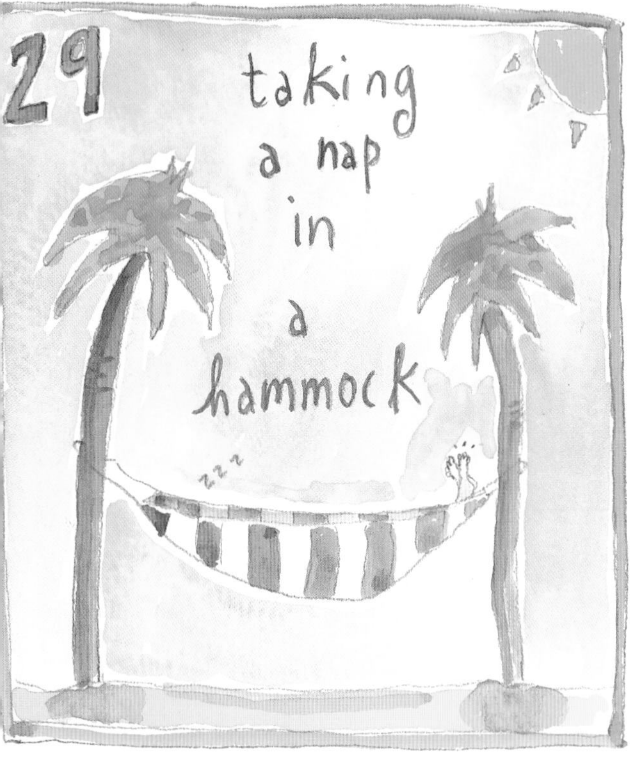
29
taking a nap in a hammock
z z z

**30** toasting marshmallows

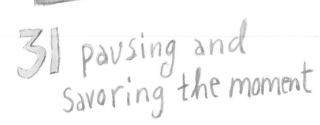

**31** pausing and savoring the moment

**32** smelling salt air

33 gliding

**34** making soup and simmering it on the stove

**35** giving yourself permission to grow

**36** taking time to smell the roses

**37** dancing with the stars

**38** curling up with a good book

39 making yourself a picnic

**40** using all the settings for recline

**41** counting your blessings

**42** watching fireflies

43 daydreaming
44 getting crafty

glue

collected stuff

45 exercising and
feeling strong

My Journal...
my thoughts and dreams and feelings

**47** going out on the water

**48** painting your toes a silly superficial color

who needs a prince pink

50

wandering down an
unexplored path

**51** Listening to the pitter-patter of

rain on the roof

**52** rocking gently in a rocking chair

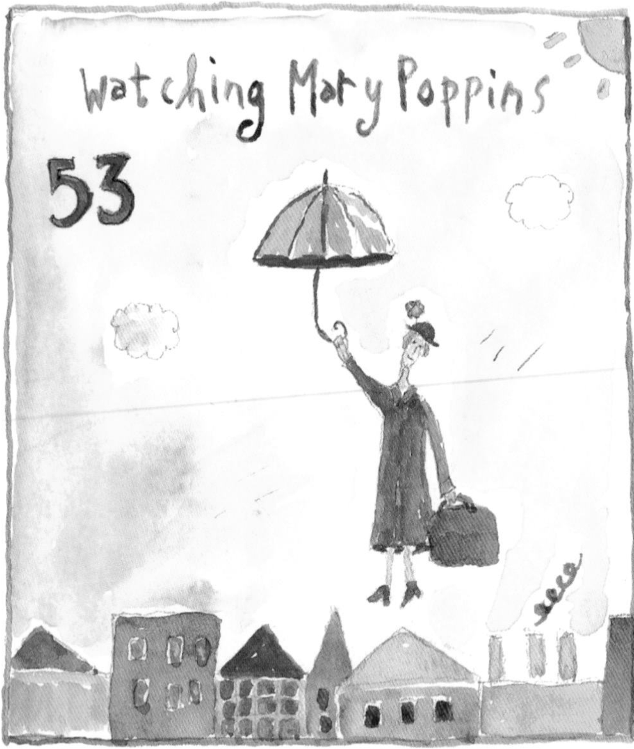
Watching Mary Poppins
53

**54** having a long talk with an old friend

**55**

Listening to a fountain burbling

**56** Watching the sunset

**57** swinging

on a porch swing

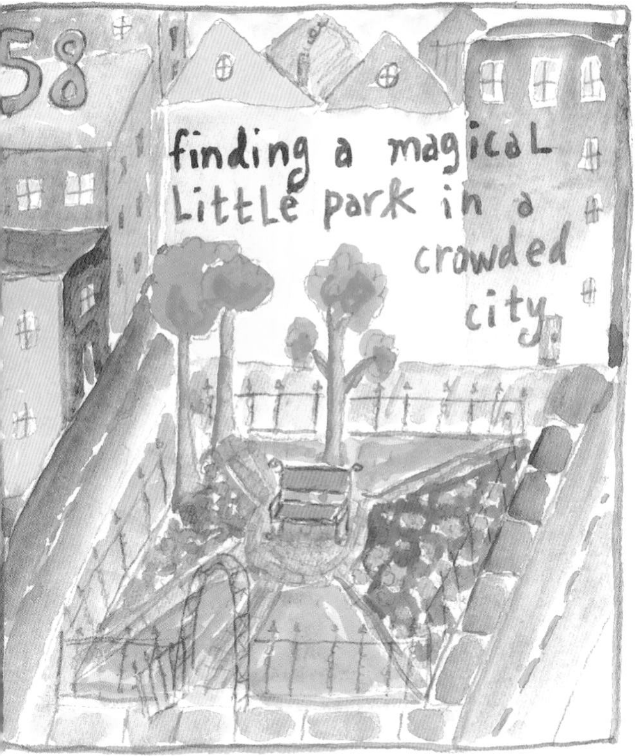
58
finding a magical
Little park in a
crowded
city

59 having a good
belly laugh

60 snuggling in for
breakfast in bed

# 61

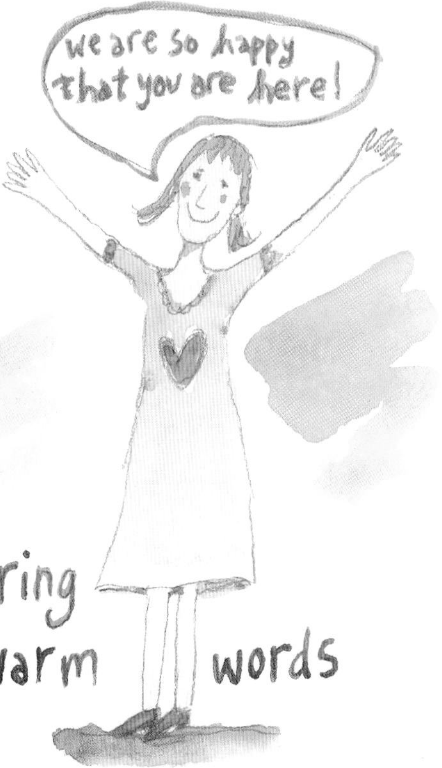


## hearing warm words

**63** being told that you are beautiful inside and out

**64**

finding the sweetness in the middle of the pie

**65** having **warm cookies** and **milk**

**66** hearing a guitar

softly strumming

67

opportunity

finding a door that opens

68 and a warm welcome within...

69 celebrating

for no reason

**71** window shopping (but knowing you have enough already)

**72** smelling the coffee brewing

**73** the phrase: "make yourself at home."

**74** getting wagged at

**75** and purred at

**76** finding a place for yourself

this is where I belong

School of the Arts

**77** savoring the scent of bread fresh out of the oven

**78** having someone say,
"I believe in you."

**79** walking in the

grass barefoot

**80** seeing the sun break through the clouds

**81** planting a seed

**82** Looking at old photographs and remembering

**83** finishing your "to do" list

I feel so much lighter!

**85** imagining angels

watching over you

86 finding a rainbow

after a storm

87 being read to

**88** strolling around in siLLy flip-flops

**89** having someone else cook you a meal

90

flying south in the winter

91 sitting and reading in companionable silence

## 92 rewarding yourself

DAY AT THE SPA COUPON
TO: ME   FROM: ME
For : A Deserved REST

## 93 going to a Diner for breakfast

FLO'S
EAT

94 choosing your
own path

my way

the main road -- -

and being
true to yourself

95 looking at the
fall foliage

96 doing something
you haven't done
in years

97 getting
smiled
at (and
smiling
back)

**98** Listening to the soothing gentle sound of wind chimes

**99** volunteering and giving back

**100** having the
story come to
a happy ending

ever · · · · after...

Other books by Sandy Gingras

*What a Woman Needs*
*I Like You*
*Lessons of a Turtle*
*Reasons to Be Happy*
*Thank You*
*Walks on the Beach*
*She Went Out on a Limb*